MANCHESTER & SALFORD IN PHOTOGRAPHS

JON SPARKS

AMBERLEY

ACKNOWLEDGEMENTS

As always, I've had fantastic support from my partner and critical friend, Bernie Carter.

I'd also like to thank individuals and establishments who granted access and in some cases went out of their way to help, especially Joe Hoyle at Victoria Baths Trust and Fergus Wilde at Chetham's Library.

For much help in identifying some of the less obvious locations, many thanks to Helen Colley. I'm only sorry I couldn't use more of them.

ABOUT THE PHOTOGRAPHER

Jon Sparks is a freelance photographer and writer specialising in the outdoors. He's known Manchester from an early age and has been based in nearby Lancashire all his working life. While he's had fantastic experiences in New Zealand, Pakistan, Jordan and other far-flung spots, many of his favourite places are much closer to home.

Alongside pure landscape photography, he's worked extensively on outdoor pursuits; in fact, he'd argue that there's no hard boundary between the two. He's tried most activities but has a special love of all things bike, whether skinny-tyred road bikes or mountain bikes. He's also a lifelong hill-walker, scrambler and 'resting' rock climber. He's picked up awards for both writing and photography, and indeed has written extensively about photography.

First published 2020

Amberley Publishing
The Hill, Stroud
Gloucestershire, GL5 4EP

www.amberley-books.com

Copyright © Jon Sparks, 2020

The right of Jon Sparks to be identified as the Author of this work has been asserted in accordance with the Copyrights, Designs and Patents Act 1988.

ISBN 978 1 4456 9834 2 (print)
ISBN 978 1 4456 9835 9 (ebook)

British Library Cataloguing in Publication Data.
A catalogue record for this book is available from the British Library.

Typesetting by SJmagic DESIGN SERVICES, India.
Printed in the UK.

INTRODUCTION

Almost all of these photos were shot within a ten-month period (April 2019–February 2020), an inevitable consequence of trying to stay current within a dynamic and rapidly changing urban landscape – and fortuitously finished just before Covid-19 lockdown descended. However, my acquaintance with Manchester and Salford goes back a lot further. Working on this book has been a journey of both discovery and rediscovery.

Earliest memories include shopping trips, by train, in the 1960s. There have been events at venues like the Free Trade Hall, Bridgewater Hall and more recently Salford Quays, and one unforgettable night in the velodrome during the 2002 Commonwealth Games. Riding that same track myself, even at half the speed of the pros, is another treasured experience.

Background research, as well as the actual photography, has renewed my awareness that Manchester and Salford have always punched above their weight in historical and cultural terms. Above all, they were the world's first industrial cities. And, as world leaders, their story is fittingly cosmopolitan. From the Romans to the Flemish weavers of the Middle Ages, offcomers have left their mark. Karl Marx and Friedrich Engels first met here. New Zealander Ernest Rutherford first split the atom in Manchester, and graphene was first isolated by two Russian-born physicists.

In the city of the world's first inter-city railway terminus, it's fitting that I reached the great majority of locations by a mix of public transport and foot-slogging. Central Manchester, in particular, has become much more walkable and pleasant to visit, thanks principally to the Metrolink, Britain's biggest and best light rail system.

Manchester skyline from Heaton Park

River Medlock, Clayton Vale

Green Salford: Chat Moss

The River Irwell and Manchester city centre

Roofscape,
Manchester
Town Hall

Civil Justice Centre, Spinningfields

The Principal (formerly Palace Hotel)

The Shakespeare,
Fountain Street

Welcom

Plymouth Grove pub, Plymouth Grove

Peveril of the Peak,
Great Bridgewater Street

Free Trade Hall (now The Edwardian hotel)

The Sawyers Arms,
Deansgate/Bridge Street

Steps of Manchester Central, looking to Midland Hotel

Maintenance worker,
Midland Hotel

Royal Exchange Theatre

Daily Express
Building
and Hudson
Buildings, Great
Ancoats Street

Contact Theatre

The Bridgewater Hall

Salford Museum and Art Gallery

John Rylands Library (University of Manchester), Deansgate

Chetham's Library

Table used by Marx and Engels, Chetham's Library

The Portico Library

Manchester Central Library

Reflection of
Manchester
Central Library

Manchester Art Gallery

The Manchester Museum

National Football Museum (Urbis Building)
from Cathedral Gardens

Whitworth
Art Gallery

People's History Museum

The Lowry, Salford Quays

Manchester Opera House,
Quay Street

THE · PLAY · MIRRORS · LIFE

Science and
Industry
Museum,
London Road

Peel Building, University of Salford

Lady Hale Building, University of Salford

Graduation Day, University of Manchester

National Graphene Institute,
University of Manchester

The Hollings Building, aka Toast Rack, University of Manchester

The Renold
Building,
University of
Manchester

University of Manchester Innovation Centre

Birley Fields campus, Manchester
Metropolitan University

Business School and John Dalton Building,
Manchester Metropolitan University

Library and Business School,
Manchester Metropolitan
University

Cancer Research
Centre, Withington

The Christie Hospital,
Withington

Salford Royal Hospital (Hope Building)

Royal Manchester Children's Hospital

Viaducts, Castlefield

Viaduct detail,
Castlefield

Barton Swing Aqueduct,
Manchester Ship Canal

Salford Quays lift
bridge (aka the
Lowry Bridge)

Trinity Bridge and the Lowry Hotel

Spinningfields Bridge

The Hulme Arch with Deansgate and Beetham Towers

Pedestrian Bridge,
Corporation Street

Liverpool Road Station, the world's first passenger railway terminus

Concourse, Piccadilly Station

Network map and war memorial, Victoria Station

Metrolink at Shudehill

The Station, Irlam

IRLAM

TELEPHONE

WELCOME TO IRLAM

Cafe
1923
Bar

Reflections and railway,
First Street

Canal Street (Rochdale Canal),
Gay Village

New Islington

The Rochdale Canal in Manchester city centre

Bridgewater Canal and the Beetham Tower

Dale Street
Warehouse,
Piccadilly Basin

Murrays' Mills and Rochdale Canal, Ancoats

Victoria Mill, Miles Platting

Tootal, Broadhurst and Lee Building
(Churchgate House), Oxford Street

Asia House,
Princess
Street

Lancaster House, Princess Street

ASIA
HOUSE

Great Northern Warehouse

Britannia Manchester
Hotel (originally
Watts Warehouse)

Cyclist on the
Lowry Bridge

Racing at Manchester Velodrome
(National Cycling Centre)

2019 Tour of Britain
on Liverpool Road

City of Manchester Stadium
(Etihad Stadium, home of
Manchester City) and The Runner

Sir Matt Busby statue, Old Trafford

Victoria Baths

Interior, Victoria Baths

Vimto Park, Granby Row

Emmeline Pankhurst
monument, St Peter's
Square

Alan Turing memorial,
Sackville Gardens

Archimedes' Eureka
Moment, former
UMIST campus

Anthony Burgess mural, Northern Quarter

WE CAN DESTROY WHAT WE HAVE WRITTEN, BUT WE CAN NOT UNWRITE IT.

ANTHONY BURGESS

A CLOCKWORK ORANGE.

@TANKPETROL

Blue Tit mural, Northern Quarter

Lion, Heaton Hall

Wicker horse, by the Rochdale Canal (below Oxford Road)

Afflecks Palace,
Northern Quarter

Chinatown Arch, Faulkner Street

Salford Cathedral

St Philip's Church, Salford

Church of the Holy Name of Jesus, Oxford Road

Manchester Cathedral

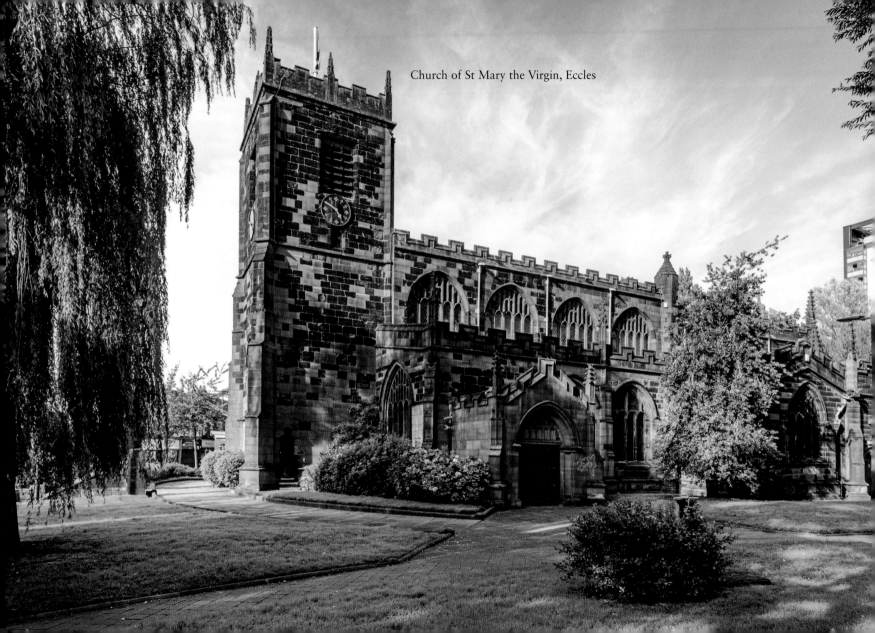

Church of St Mary the Virgin, Eccles

The Edgar Wood Centre, Fallowfield

Ordsall Hall, Salford

Kersal Cell, Salford

Wythenshawe Hall

Clayton Hall

Elizabeth Gaskell's House,
Plymouth Grove

The Green Building, New Wakefield Street

Gateway House, Piccadilly Station
Approach (CIS Tower in distance)

Albert Hall, Quay Street

St Ann's Square,
decorated for
Chinese New Year

Barton Arcade

Printworks

Shambles Square

House of Fraser (formerly Kendals/
Kendal Milne)

Christmas
Market and
Town Hall,
Albert Square

Spinningfields

Walkway beside National Football
Museum, Cathedral Gardens

Buskers, Market Street

Reconstructed Roman
Gateway, Mamucium

100 King Street, formerly
the Midland Bank

15–17 King Street

Lawrence Buildings, Mount Street

Deansgate and
Quay Street

Bridgewater House, Whitworth Street, and Deansgate Towers

One Angel Square

Manchester Central and
Peterloo memorial

The Lowry, Salford Quays

MediaCityUK, Salford Quays

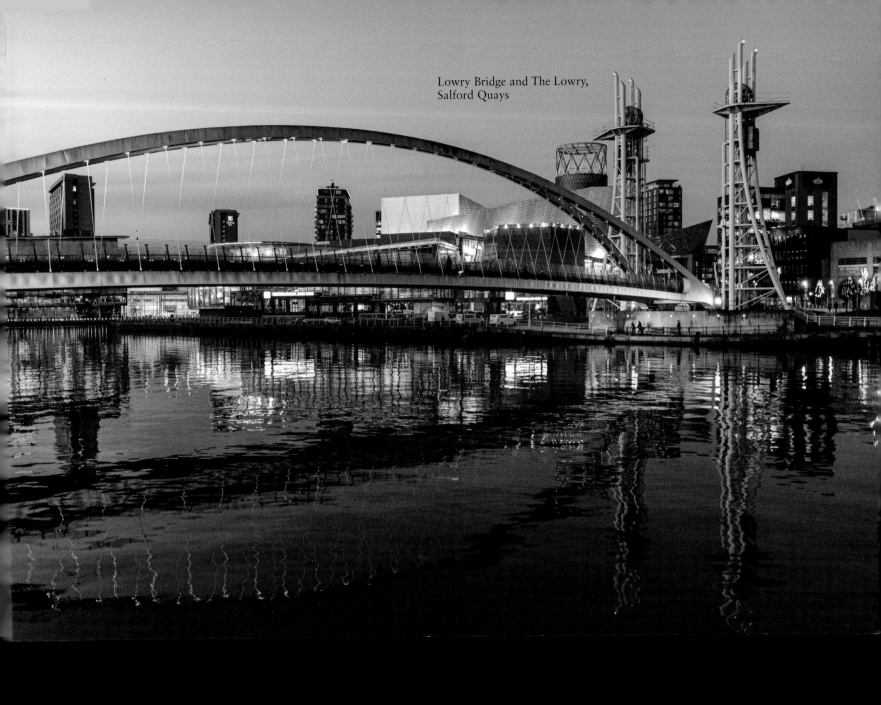

Lowry Bridge and The Lowry,
Salford Quays

MediaCityUK and The Lowry, Salford Quays